The Brit
Rail Network

1974–78

ARTHUR WILSON

BRITAIN'S RAILWAYS SERIES, VOLUME 60

Front cover image: On 26 May 1977, 40112 heads an empty hopper wagon train east through Manchester Victoria station.

Title page image: 47474 heads an intermodal for the docks at Southampton west through Eastleigh station on 23 June 1976.

Contents page image: 31314 is seen on empty passenger coaching stock at Yarmouth Vauxhall station on 9 June 1975.

Back cover image: On 8 June 1976, a Class 20 pairing of 20146/138 gets underway away from Falkland yard in Ayr with a northbound mixed freight train.

About the Author

In the 1950s my family moved to Prestwick from Kilmarnock. Our house overlooked the former Glasgow and South Western line (G&SW) from Glasgow St Enoch station (later Glasgow Central station) to Ayr and Stranraer. At secondary school, a number of my contemporaries were trainspotters, and this is where my interest in the railways began.

After graduating from Glasgow University with a degree in chemistry, I worked initially in the Glasgow area, and in the late 1970s moved to Haslingden, Lancashire. My home location enabled me to visit the railways in the Manchester and Derby areas. In later years, I had the benefit of a railway employee pass, which provided an opportunity to visit large areas of the network.

My first camera was a Box Brownie, however, the results left a little to be desired, especially with fast-moving trains. After experimenting with a number of cameras, I switched to a Canon AT-1 and then a Canon T70. In terms of film, I used Kodak at first, followed by Agfa and then Jessops slide film from 1980 onwards. In 2003, I went digital and bought a Canon EOS 400D; today I use a Canon EOS 750D.

This text focuses on the British Rail (BR) blue years, when we had a variety of locomotives and rolling stock, and each of the regions had distinct motive power. I have tried to include as much as possible. All the photos were

taken pre-internet and some lack specific details. Back then, I would simply turn up at a location and given enough time, something interesting would appear before the lens!

I wish to acknowledge the tremendous help and assistance given to me by my friend Stuart Fowler in the preparation of this book.

Western Class 52 D1028 named *Western Hussar* is seen at Newport station with a passenger service for Cardiff Central from London Paddington on 3 October 1974. Note the slight escape of steam from the pipe at the front of the locomotive.

Published by Key Books
An imprint of Key Publishing Ltd
PO Box 100
Stamford
Lincs PE9 1XQ

www.keypublishing.com

The right of Arthur Wilson to be identified as the author of this book has been asserted in accordance with the Copyright, Designs and Patents Act 1988 Sections 77 and 78.

Copyright © Arthur Wilson, 2024

ISBN 978 1 80282 788 0

Typeset by SJmagic DESIGN SERVICES, India.

Contents

Chapter 1
Scotland

Taken on 18 August 1976, a Swindon Works Class 126 diesel multiple unit (DMU) at Stranraer Harbour station having arrived with the 08:25 service from Glasgow Central. The view includes the signal box. A Sealink vessel is berthed at the dock for a sailing to Belfast, Northern Ireland. Sealink UK Ltd was sold to Sea Containers by the government in 1984, and in 1990, the service was taken over by Stena Line. The last sailing from Stranraer Harbour to Belfast was in November 2011, when Stena moved up the coast to a new £200 million development at Cairnryan. The harbour area remains derelict with a basic DMU service operating from Ayr or Kilmarnock to the Harbour station.

25213 approaches Stranraer Harbour station on 18 August 1976 with a rake of parcel vans including two general utility vans (GUVs) and an ex London Midland and Scottish coach. The vans were unloaded at the station with the mail going forward to Belfast by Sealink.

Stranraer Town station is seen on 18 August 1976 with the empty Mk1 stock off the overnight service from London Euston stabled for cleaning and servicing. Stranraer Town station closed to passengers on 7 March 1966. The stub of line heading south was the line to Portpatrick, which closed on 25 September 1950.

Swindon Works Class 126 DMU three-coach set formed of 51031/59404/51012 sits at Girvan station with the 11:10 service to Ayr on 2 September 1976. The centre coach, 59404, is now part of the preserved Class 126 set at the Bo'ness and Kinneil Railway (BKR) near Falkirk. Class 126 DMUs were introduced to Ayrshire line services based at Ayr depot in August 1959; by the 1980s the sets had covered two million miles in service, with the last two units withdrawn in January 1983. Girvan station was rebuilt after fire damage in 1946. It is now a category B listed structure as an example of an early post-war railway station in the modern (Art Deco) style.

25008 heads a mixed parcels and empty oil tanks (for fuelling BR Sealink vessels at Stranraer) from Stranraer to Falkland yard out of Ayr station on 9 June 1977. The combined station and hotel at Ayr was set on fire in 2023 and faces an uncertain future; at the time of writing, a large part of the hotel has now been demolished.

A pair of Class 20s in the shape of 20223/138 are seen coming down the line from Annbank at Blackhouse Junction on the approach to Newton-on-Ayr with a loaded merry-go-round (MGR) from Killoch to Longannet Power Station on 26 December 1974.

25083 heads a loaded coal train formed of 16-ton wagons off the Mauchline line, passing Ayr depot and heading into Falkland yard on 29 March 1978. Ayr depot, coded 67C, opened in 1879 and was designed by Andrew Galloway. Around 1966, it closed to steam and became a diesel maintenance depot for locos and DMUs. The depot closed in 2007; track lifting and demolition took place in 2019, and the site is now derelict. Visible behind the depot is Somerset Park, the home of Ayr United Football Club.

40009 heads a parcels train for Carlisle (via the line to Mauchline and the G&SW) through Newton-on-Ayr station on 25 July 1977.

Left: 20117 brings the breakdown train from Ayr depot to Ayr harbour on 7 April 1977 to re-rail a Class 08 shunter, which had derailed in the harbour sidings. The small signal box visible in the background controlled access via a straight crossing to the original G&SW Ayr station, which opened on 5 August 1839. That station closed to passengers on 1 July 1857, and a station opened at Townhead close to the present station, which opened in 1886. The site of the original G&SW station became a goods station; it closed around 1970 and was demolished in 1979, and has been replaced by housing and a supermarket.

Below: 08144 brings a mixture of wagons in from Falkland yard to the sidings at Ayr harbour on 29 September 1975. In the background are rakes of 16-ton coal wagons, the coal being loaded on to boats by tipping the contents of a loaded wagon into them. The coal was exported to Northern Ireland.

On 9 August 1974, Class 20s 20120/103 head a rake of empty 16-ton coal wagons out of the sidings at Ayr harbour, likely bound for Dunaskin.

26028 heads a long rake of loaded 16-ton coal wagons north out of Falkland yard, with the signal box that controlled the signals and the points visible on the west side of the yard on 28 March 1975. Since the demise of coal traffic, the yard is now deserted, with only the occasional test train or engineering train stabling on the east side. The former staff offices also located on the east side have long been demolished.

Class 27/1 27111 heads a fitted freight out of Falkland yard bound for the Glasgow area on 6 April 1977. This Class 27 was one of 24 fitted with dual brakes (vacuum and air) and re-classified as 27/1s. They retained their train-heating boiler for working top and tail (later with 27/2 conversions) with six dual-heat Mk2 coaches on Edinburgh to Glasgow services.

37100 heads empty liquid ammonia tank train 6E56 from the ICI Nylon Plant at Ardeer back to Haverton Hill in the north-east of England on 13 July 1974. Note the barrier wagon behind the locomotive. The nylon plant at the Ardeer site opened in 1969 and closed around 1981.

40198 heads 1E37, the Saturdays-only return working from Largs in Scotland to Newcastle, south through Prestwick on 29 June 1974. The photo was taken from the road bridge over the railway at Maryborough Road.

Class 24 24107 and Class 25 25244 with two parcels vans head north through Prestwick, running from Ayr to Kilmarnock on 19 April 1976.

20036 is involved in track-relaying work with a crane just south of Prestwick station on 27 July 1975. The photo was taken from the railway footbridge at Bridge Street. Compared with the safety clothing and other equipment worn by track workers today, there is little evidence of much safety equipment in use apart from the odd orange vest.

Above: 47045 with a rake of Mk1 stock heads the 15:00 service from Carlisle to Stranraer Harbour, passing the site of what is now Prestwick Airport station (opened on 5 September 1994) on 1 July 1977. The opening of the airport's station resulted in Prestwick station being renamed Prestwick Town station.

Left: On 17 August 1974, 27025 heads a mixed freight from Carlisle north through Kilmarnock station, then into the freight yard at Kilmarnock (now a site owned by Brodie Engineering and Morrisons supermarket).

08104 outbased from Carlisle Kingmoor, and 45057 with a Mk1 coach, are seen stabled in the north bays at Dumfries station on 1 June 1977. Following the closure of the Port Road between Dumfries and Stranraer on 14 June 1965, the bay platforms, which were used for Stranraer services, were often used to stable locos and at least one Class 08 shunter. Class 45 locos were common on the G&SW line, working the Thames Clyde express and Leeds services. The bays have now been filled in and are used for car parking and collections.

25228 shunts the empty stock of a Scottish Railway Preservation Society (SRPS) special from Burntisland to Largs on 21 May 1977, with a view of the signal box controlling the signals and points at Largs in the image. The passengers, on arrival, sailed on the TS *Queen Mary*, built in 1933, and affectionately called 'The Glasgow Boat', having sailed daily from the Broomielaw. The TS *Queen Mary* was retired in 1977.

27032 and 27044 are stabled on empty coaching stock at Largs station on 12 March 1977, in order to work the return of a preview special from the London-Midland region. These trains ran to give people a sight of Largs as a holiday destination. The Class 27s would likely come off at Falkland yard, to be replaced by a Class 40 or 47.

A line up of DMUs stabled at Largs station on 12 June 1976. From left to right are a Metro-Cammell unit Class 101, a Derby Suburban three-car unit Class 116 and two Derby Works three-car Class 107 units.

A view of the iron ore-loading terminal at General Terminus Quay in Govan with 08726 stabled and another unidentified Class 08 on the right on 8 July 1977. This site opened in 1958 to handle imported iron ore from vessels, which came up the River Clyde. The iron ore was discharged directly into 33-ton hoppers and taken by pairs of Class 20s to the steelworks in Lanarkshire, mainly Ravenscraig. As ships became larger, the riverside location became more difficult to access and so a deep-water port was built at Hunterston, off the Largs line, to handle the imported iron ore. General Terminus Quay was closed in 1979.

Some of the platforms at Glasgow Central station, on 19 June 1976, have DMU sets stabled, as well as Class 303 electric multiple unit (EMU) 303040 and Class 311 311099 about to depart to the destination of Hamilton as noted on the roller blind. In total, 91 Class 303 EMUs were built by Pressed Steel at Linwood near Paisley in two lots from 1959 to 1961. The first 35 were built for the North Clyde line and the remainder for the Cathcart Circle. The final units were withdrawn from service on 30 August 2002. 303032 is now preserved at the BKR, with its motor coach taken from 303023. An additional 19 Class 311 EMUs were built by Cravens in Sheffield in 1967 following the Inverclyde electrification and all were withdrawn by 1990. Two sets (311103/104) were converted to work for Sandite duties, renumbered 936103/104, and were withdrawn in 1999. In 2002, Railtrack donated 936103 to the Summerlee Heritage Park at Coatbridge; one of the driving cars, 76414, was later scrapped.

BR Blue 303066 arrives at Glasgow Central station with a service from Cathcart on 19 June 1976.

Clayton Class 17 D8574, with three others behind it, is seen condemned and awaiting scrapping at British Rail Engineering Ltd (BREL) Glasgow Works, on a visit on 9 August 1975. I counted 22 other Class 17s for scrapping that day. D8574 was built by the Clayton Equipment Company Ltd at Hatton, Derby, and allocated new to Haymarket on 31 January 1964. It later moved to Polmadie depot on 1 March 1969, before withdrawal on 31 December 1971. It was cut up in September 1975.

Class 27/2 27210 heads Mk2 stock with a Class 27/1 on the rear at Glasgow Queen Street station with a morning service to Edinburgh Waverley on 27 July 1974. As the Mk2 stock was dual (steam and electric) heated it was decided that 12 Class 27/1s would be converted to electric train heating by removing the boiler of each and replacing it with a Deutz eight-cylinder air-cooled diesel engine and alternator, which were known to catch fire. Additional vents were later cut in the bodyside to improve cooling. 27210 was converted from D5409, and later renumbered 27064 when it was removed from the Edinburgh to Glasgow duties.

A general view of Oban station (opened 30 June 1880) and harbour on 14 June 1976, with the fuel tanks used to fuel the Caledonian MacBrayne shipping fleet operating out of Oban visible on the tracks near the quayside, along with a Class 25 in the station.

27020 departs Oban with the 12:25 service to Glasgow Queen Street station comprised of Mk1 stock, on 14 June 1976, as the second man prepares to accept the token from the signalman. Radio Electronic Token Block signalling is now used to control the West Highland Line.

Above: This was the scene at Mallaig on 21 August 1976, of 27038 awaiting departure on a return SRPS railtour, which departed at 16:22 to Glasgow Queen Street. A locomotive change was encountered at Fort William, with 27111 taking over for the journey to Glasgow.

Left: Inverness-based Class 24s 24117 and 24126 with steam heating on the Mk1 coaching stock working well, are seen at Stirling station on 1 October 1975, operating the 09:35 Glasgow Queen Street to Inverness service. Inverness-based Class 24s were not that common on services to Inverness from Glasgow Queen Street.

27008 is seen at Stirling station, working the 11:52 service ex Dundee to Glasgow Queen Street with Mk1 stock on 26 September 1975. This Class 27 was the last to be withdrawn on 13 August 1987.

40160, with headcode 6B89, is seen at Stirling station with the 12:15 Inverness to Glasgow Queen Street service on 26 September 1975.

Right: A six-car Class 101 DMU set (2x3) departs Stirling station for Edinburgh Waverley on 26 September 1975 and passes the goods yard with several vans present to serve the John Player cigarette factory, which closed in 1983. The steam engine shed (65J), which closed in 1966, was also located close by, on the same side as the yard.

Below: Class 47 47273, with headcode 1E17, heads a passenger train for London King's Cross south through Ladybank station from Aberdeen on 27 July 1974.

47525 approaches Kirkcaldy station on 13 May 1977 with a service from Aberdeen to Edinburgh Waverley, which was due at Kirkcaldy at 12:58. The area still retained much semaphore signalling in this era.

This 13 May 1977 scene finds 06002 with a guard's van shunting the goods yard at Kirkcaldy. The stove in the guard's van is lit as can be seen from the smoke. The Class 06 would also be used on the harbour branch at Kirkcaldy, which closed in 1984.

47273 departs Kirkcaldy station on 13 May 1977 with the 10:20 service to Inverness from Edinburgh Waverley, formed of a long rake of Mk1 and Mk2 coaches, which were typical of long-distance passenger workings of the time.

26009 heads a parcels train for Edinburgh Waverley past Haymarket depot on 19 July 1975. Note the abundance of semaphore signalling in the area.

On 8 November 1975, 40070, with steam heating working well, is seen at Edinburgh Waverley station with the 09:50 service to Plymouth. I took this train as far as York, and at Newcastle station the Class 40 was replaced by 46054. Note the Brute trolley loaded with parcels.

Left: 83013 heads a mixed freight north through Carstairs station towards Mossend yard on 15 September 1976. The extensive station buildings were demolished and replaced with a single combined ticket office/toilet and waiting area.

Below: 40081 is seen bringing in the Edinburgh portion of a train for Birmingham into Carstairs on 15 September 1976, where it will be combined with the 10:35 Glasgow to Birmingham New Street hauled by 86205.

Chapter 2

Midland Region

87007 is seen heading the 10:45 London Euston to Glasgow Central service on the approach to Carlisle on 4 October 1974. This passenger service was known as the Royal Scot, having been introduced in May 1974, with a new five-hour schedule to and from Glasgow Central to London Euston with only one stop at Preston. The Class 87s were built between 1973 and 1975 at BREL Works in Crewe.

On 18 April 1975, 31178/31137 double-head a loaded iron ore train from Teesside to Workington, and is seen on the freight avoiding line at Carlisle heading towards Currock Junction, about to pass the wagon repair works at Currock on the left. The steel plant closed in August 2006 after producing steel rails for 129 years.

25051 heads a mixed freight on 18 April 1975 south from Kingmoor yard at Carlisle on the freight avoiding line. This line was electrified at the same time as the West Coast Main Line (WCML). On 1 May 1984, a freightliner service approaching Carlisle had dragging brakes, which were subsequently isolated. However, on restarting the train it unfortunately divided, resulting in the rear portion running out of control following the train itself. The front portion arrived safely in Carlisle station and a signalman, realising a collision in the station was likely, routed the rear portion on to the freight avoiding line. The runaway freight wagons derailed on Caldew Bridge, destroying the southern part of it and some of the payload polluted the river. The freight avoiding line never reopened and eventually the track was lifted. All freight services since then have been booked through the station.

47444 heads a southbound freight from Carlisle Kingmoor yard into Workington on 10 August 1976, passing the lovely mix of semaphores.

Above: Derby Works DMU Driving Trailer Composite M56243 and Motor Brake Second M50959, introduced into service in 1959, depart Workington with the 11:00 service to Carlisle on 10 August 1976.

Right: Class 37s 37194/006 double-head iron ore train 6M33 from Teesside into Workington, heading for the steel plant on 10 August 1976.

In dire light, Cravens DMU Motor Composite M50795 and Motor Brake Second M50762 are seen at Windermere station with the 13:55 service to Oxenholme station on 3 April 1976. The single track was cut back to a new truncated station in 1986 following demolition of the train shed.

Metro-Cammell DMU E50271/E59532/E50284 is seen at Morecambe Promenade station with a working from Leeds on 6 April 1976. Morecambe Promenade station was opened in 1907 by the Midland Railway and closed in February 1994. After a 12-week break in service, a new Morecambe station was opened on a site closer to the town centre.

84009 heads a mail train south at Lancaster on 7 April 1976. The Class 84s were built by the North British Locomotive Company between 1960 and 1961, only ten were built and the last was withdrawn in 1980.

82003 heads a fascinatingly mixed parcels train north through Lancaster station on 27 May 1977. The Class 82s were designed by Metropolitan Vickers and produced by Beyer Peacock Ltd on behalf of British Rail between 1960 and 1962. Only eight were built, with most being placed in store during 1982 and the majority withdrawn by 1983. Note that 82005 and 82008 were reinstated for use on empty coaching stock between London Euston and Willesden sidings.

Right: 25198 heads a short parcels train, consisting of two ex-Southern Region-designed vans, south at Preston station on 6 April 1976.

Below: On 26 May 1977, 40009 was whistling through Preston station as it headed a tank train north.

25144 heads a rake of ballast wagons north through a rather deserted Preston station on 26 May 1977. The train consist was typical of the era with a mixture of catfish and dogfish wagons in tow.

Birmingham Railway Carriage and Wagon Company DMU 50525/59181/50493 is seen stabled at Blackpool North station on 8 April 1976. The station was opened in its present form in 1974 following decommissioning and demolition of the main station buildings, train shed and platforms. The 1938 excursion platform canopy building was refurbished to become the new main station.

On 27 May 1977, 31159 on empty limestone wagons, is seen at Hellifield, waiting to head towards Leeds.

Split box 40125 heads a mixed freight train through Hellifield from Carlisle Kingmoor on 27 May 1977. The train will take the Clitheroe freight-only line from here to join the WCML south of Preston at Farington Curve Junction. The Class 40 would probably have been replaced by an electric loco at Farington.

45013 heads a Glasgow Central to Leeds passenger train south at Hellifield on a warm and sunny 27 May 1977.

Cravens DMU 50757/50790 is seen at Colne station with the 12:42 service to Preston on 6 April 1976. Colne is now a terminus station but used to continue on to join the line to Leeds and Carlisle at Skipton. This line was closed in February 1970. There has been a long campaign for it to be reinstated.

40139 heads the 11:55 Saturdays-only Blackpool North to Bradford Exchange passenger train through Accrington station on 19 August 1978.

37105 heads the Saturdays-only 1M06 09:23 Sheffield to Blackpool North service near Rose Grove on 19 August 1978.

45016 heads a loaded coal train at Blackburn station on 6 April 1976. The loco backed the train into the yard before heading off light engine. Note the mill chimneys, which were a prominent feature of the landscape in the area.

40116 heads a freight train formed of COVHOP wagons with alumina traffic north on the WCML at Wigan on 9 April 1976. The photo was taken from Wigan Wallgate station.

25192 heads a mixed freight formed of mineral wagons, gunpowder vans and brake vans west down from Miles Platting, approaching Manchester Victoria station on 26 May 1977.

Right: 40055 heads a loaded steel train west through Manchester Victoria station on 26 May 1977. Note the London Midland Railway totem for Manchester Victoria station on the left of the photo.

Below: Class 504 Manchester to Bury two-car set with 77177 leading, heads for Manchester Victoria station from Bury Bolton Street station on 29 May 1978. Railway operations on the Bury line ended on 17 August 1991 in order for the line to be converted to Metrolink operation.

Class 76 EM1 Bo-Bo 76052 heads a freight east through Dinting station on the Woodhead line, probably bound for Wath yard on 17 May 1977. How times change! Railway workers on the line next to a live track would be unheard of these days, especially without a hard hat and contemporary protective equipment.

Class 76s EM1 Bo-Bo 76006/76027 head a loaded MGR coal train ex-Wath yard west through Dinting station bound for Fiddlers Ferry Power Station near Warrington on 17 May 1977. The 76s would come off the train in the yard near Guide Bridge, to be replaced by a Class 40 or 47 diesel locomotive for the onward journey to Fiddlers Ferry. The Woodhead route, energised at 1500 volts DC, closed east of Hadfield on 18 July 1981.

Class 506 Manchester–Glossop–Hadfield three-car set (introduced in 1954) 59405/59505/59605 heads a working from Hadfield station to Manchester Piccadilly at Dinting station on 17 May 1977. These units, along with the Class 76s, were maintained at Reddish depot, which closed in April 1983. In December 1984, the Glossop line was converted to the standard 25kV AC overhead system and the Class 506 EMUs were withdrawn and replaced by Class 303 EMUs from the Glasgow area.

85006 heads a colourful loaded car train south at Crewe on 1 June 1977. Today, most car trains utilise covered car wagons to prevent damage or vandalism.

25089 heads a loaded limestone train from the Derbyshire quarries off the line from Derby and north through Crewe station on 9 April 1976.

On 9 April 1976, 24052 shunts stores vans at Crewe station.

81005 is seen at Crewe Works after overhaul along with 86030 awaiting painting on 24 September 1977. The Class 81s were built by Associated Electrical Industries at the Birmingham Railway Carriage and Wagon Company (BRCW) at Smethwick between 1959 and 1964 and all were taken out of service by 1991.

Class 502 EMU with car M29890M leading is seen at Liverpool Exchange station, working the 16:53 service to Ormskirk on 29 April 1977. Liverpool Exchange station closed on 30 April 1977 and the replacement Moorfields station opened on 2 May 1977. Within a few years, Liverpool Exchange station was demolished.

47280 heads a loaded MGR coal train east through Chester station on 7 October 1975, likely from the Point of Ayr Colliery.

Above: Class 103 Park Royal DMUs 56155/56163/50400/50405 with a train to Llandudno are seen approaching Rhyl on 20 March 1976. The Class 103s were ordered from British United Transport and built at the Crossley Motor Works in Stockport, introduced in 1957, and withdrawn by 1983.

Left: 47487 heads a passenger train from London Euston to Holyhead non-stop through Rhyl at 14:35 on 20 March 1976. The Class 47 would have taken over from an electric loco at Crewe.

On 19 May 1977, Class 25 25164 and Class 24 24081 head an iron ore train out of the loading terminal at Bidston Docks up the Wrexham line to the former John Summers & Sons steelworks on the Dee estuary at Shotton. The steelworks was absorbed into British Steel Corporation in 1967.

1938-built Class 503 EMU M28686M/M29716M/M29285M is seen at Bidston station with a train for West Kirby ex Liverpool Central. In addition, 1956-built Class 503 EMU M29138M/M29821M/M28375M is seen approaching the station with a train for Liverpool Central ex-West Kirby on 19 May 1977. The semaphore signal is off for the West Kirby line, with the line to Wrexham branching off to the left. The units were built by Metro-Cammell and BRCW and all were withdrawn by 1985.

25294 heads a stone train north through Shrewsbury station on 9 April 1976. The wagons for the train, interestingly, were formed of ex-London North Eastern Region 13-ton opens.

Class 304/1 EMU 009 is seen at Longport, heading for Stoke with a service from Manchester Piccadilly on 7 October 1975. The Class 304 EMUs were AC EMUs designed and produced at British Rail's Wolverton Works, and were in service between 1960 and 1996.

24091 is seen in Cockshute yard at Stoke on 1 June 1977. The days of the Class 24s were coming to an end at this point with only a handful left in service.

45110 heads 1M70, the 09:35 Carlisle to Nottingham passenger train, into Derby station on 23 July 1977.

45058 is seen at Derby station while working a Cardiff to Newcastle service on 23 July 1977.

46017 on a 1M25 09:35 Paignton to Derby passenger service arrives at Derby station from the Birmingham direction on 23 July 1977.

Class 44s 44002/005 are seen preparing to depart Derby station at 07:00 with railtour 1Z33 to Newcastle as far as York on 24 July 1977. The Class 44s, built at Derby Works between 1959 and 1960, were withdrawn between 1976 and 1980.

Class 31s 31117/31149 with the 1V88 10:10 Newcastle to Cardiff passenger train enter Derby station on 5 August 1978.

45125 heads a Sheffield Midland to London St Pancras service at Derby station on 27 November 1976.

Above: 40169 heads a freight train consisting of tube and coal wagons, south on the mainline at Westhouses on 14 September 1978.

Right: On 14 September 1978, 56048 is seen heading a southbound empty passenger coaching stock move at Westhouses.

46054 heads an MGR coal train south through Alfreton and Mansfield Parkway station on 31 May 1978.

56031 is seen stabled on Tarmac stone hoppers in the yard at Coalville during an open day on 20 August 1978.

45108 heads a passenger train for London St Pancras into Loughborough station on 24 July 1977.

56008 heads a railtour titled the *Melton Mowbray Pieman* from Barnsley to Melton Mowbray on 24 July 1977 on the approach to Loughborough station. The 56 only worked between Barnsley and Leicester.

Class 20s 20009/20005 are seen approaching Nottingham, passing the parcels depot (this was the former Nottingham London Road Low Level station, which was closed to passengers in 1944), working the 1M35 13:02 Skegness to Derby service on 8 July 1978. Pairs of Class 20s were a common sight during the summer, working services from Burton and Derby to Skegness and back.

45146 departs London Euston station with a passenger train for Sheffield on 26 June 1976. This service would usually leave from St Pancras but was diverted due to a derailment.

Class 310 EMU 093 arrives into London Euston station with an outer suburban service on 26 June 1976. These were built at Derby Carriage and Wagon Works between 1965 and 1967, and were the first EMUs to be built based on the British Rail Mk2 coach design.

Class 501 EMU 61164/75164/60164 depart London Euston station for Watford Junction on 26 June 1976. The Class 501 EMUs were built at Eastleigh Works between 1955 and 1956 for use on the former London North Western Railway/London Midland and Scottish suburban electric network of the London Midland Region. In total, 57 three-car units were built and entered service between 1957 and 1958 and were withdrawn in 1985. The units worked on lines electrified at 630V DC between London Euston and Watford Junction, services to Richmond from Broad Street station and the Croxley Green branch.

86215 at London Euston station with the 15:45 service to Glasgow Central via Kilmarnock on 22 June 1974. At Carlisle station, the Class 86 was replaced by a Class 50 for the journey up the G&SW line to Kilmarnock and Glasgow Central.

Chapter 3

Eastern Region

Metro-Cammell Class 101 DMU 50199/56077 is seen approaching Haltwhistle station with a service from Alston on 28 February 1976. It then worked the 11:50 return to Alston.

On 28 February 1976, Metro-Cammell Class 101 DMU 50199/56077 is seen at Alston station after arrival from Haltwhistle. This line closed on 3 May 1976, with the final train running on the first of that month. The South Tynedale Railway rebuilt a station at Alston and operates a 2ft-gauge line as far as Slaggyford.

On 4 April 1977, Deltic Class 55 55007, named *Pinza,* heads a passenger train for Edinburgh Waverley at Newcastle station from London King's Cross. In total, 22 Deltic locomotives were built by English Electric between 1961 and 1962 at the Vulcan Foundry in Newton-le Willows and each was fitted with two Napier Deltic D18-25 engines. The locomotives were withdrawn between January 1980 and December 1981.

On 4 April 1977, 47417 is seen with a passenger train from Edinburgh Waverley to London King's Cross at Newcastle station. 47417 came off the train here and was replaced by 47430. Note the Newcastle station nameboard still in North Eastern orange.

40009 is seen after arrival at Newcastle station with a terminating service from Liverpool Lime Street on 22 February 1975.

On 4 April 1977, 03094 is seen shunting parcels stock at Newcastle station.

37072 heads a short coal train from the Hartlepool area past Thornaby station into the yard on 22 February 1975.

On 16 April 1975, 37069 heads oil tanks out of Thornaby yard past the station at Thornaby.

55010 named *The King's Own Scottish Borderer* is seen at York station with a passenger train for London King's Cross on 27 March 1976.

Above: Class 25s 25036/25067 head 1Z32, the 08:28 London St Pancras to York railtour, on the approach to York station on 22 April 1978.

Left: 31409 arrives into Doncaster station with a passenger train from Hull Paragon on 17 March 1977.

BRCW Class 104 DMU 50554/59211/50575 is seen with a parcels van attached at Doncaster station on 6 August 1977. The Class 104 DMUs were introduced in 1957, with the last vehicle withdrawn in 1993.

On 28 March 1976, in the south bays at Doncaster station, we see Cravens Class 105 DMU 50388/56120 working the 14:16 to Sheffield Midland, while BRCW Class 110 DMU 51844/59190/59708/51826 is awaiting its next turn of duty.

47406, having departed platform 3 at Doncaster station, heads a passenger train south to London King's Cross on 28 March 1976.

Above: On 17 March 1977, 08131 heads a transfer freight south through Doncaster station to the yards close to Doncaster depot.

Left: 40038 heads an MGR coal train off the Mexborough/Sheffield line north towards Doncaster on 24 September 1976.

Below: 55019 *Royal Highland Fusilier* heads a northbound passenger train from London King's Cross towards Doncaster station on 24 September 1976.

Baby Deltic Class 23 D5901 is seen in its original livery at Doncaster Works for scrapping on 28 March 1976. Ten Class 23 locomotives were built by the English Electric Company in 1959 with a Napier Deltic T9-29 engine and were withdrawn from service between 1968 and 1971. D5901 was transferred to the departmental fleet of the Railway Technical Centre in 1969 and worked test trains until 1975; it was cut up in 1977.

Hull Paragon station features in this photo taken on 24 September 1976, with Swindon Works Class 124 Trans-Pennine DMU (Motor Composite vehicle 51953 leading) and Cravens Class 105 DMU (Motor Brake second vehicle 50372 leading,) stabled awaiting their next turn of duty. The Class 124 DMUs were introduced in 1960 and scrapped in 1984.

Class 76s 76022/025 head a westbound coal train from Wath yard and are seen approaching Penistone station on the Woodhead line on 29 March 1976. For the Class 76, designated EM1, a prototype was built at London North Eastern Railway Doncaster Works in 1941, which became E26000. Another 57 were built at the Gorton Locomotive Works in Manchester between 1950 and 1953. All were withdrawn by 1981 and scrapped between 1981 and 1983 except 76020, which is preserved at the National Railway Museum in York.

08075 is seen on a works train in the hump yard at Tinsley on 13 November 1977. The arrival sidings and hump were closed in December 1984.

47028 heads a diverted passenger train past the yard at Tinsley on 13 November 1977. Visible in the background are locomotives stabled on Tinsley depot.

13003 is stabled outside the repair shed at Tinsley depot on 13 November 1977. With the introduction of the hump yard at Tinsley, a more powerful shunter was required, so three Class 13s were built, utilising Class 08 shunters at Darlington Works of British Rail in 1965. This Class 13 comprised a master unit (ex-D4188) and a slave unit (ex-D3698). 13003 was withdrawn in January 1985 and scrapped in September 1986 at Doncaster Works. Tinsley depot closed near the end of March 1998 and was demolished by March 1999.

Class 25s 25239/107 are seen departing Sheffield Midland station with 1E34, the 09:19 Saturdays-only service (ex-Manchester Piccadilly) to Yarmouth Vauxhall on 15 July 1978.

The driver is seen climbing aboard 45145 at Sheffield Midland station on 28 March 1976 to work a passenger service to London St Pancras.

On 15 September 1978, 47307 heads a loaded MGR coal train east approaching Worksop station. The train is likely to be bound for either Cottam or West Burton coal-fired power stations.

On 15 September 1978, 56013 heads an empty MGR coal train ex-Cottam or West Burton coal-fired power stations west through Worksop station.

Derby Works Class 116 DMU 50830/59332/50880 is seen at Welwyn Garden City station with a passenger train for Royston on 8 January 1977. The Class 116 DMUs were built at Derby Litchurch Lane Works between 1957 and 1961.

313025 plus another unidentified unit is seen at Welwyn Garden City station with a passenger train for Moorgate on 8 January 1977. The Class 313 EMUs were built between February 1976 and April 1977 at BREL York Holgate Road carriage works and the remaining units in traffic were withdrawn in 2023. The inner suburban line to Welwyn Garden City was electrified in 1976. Only in 1978 was electrification completed to Royston.

Above: 31016 (nicknamed 'toffee apples' or 'skinhead' due to the roof profile lacking headcode boxes), 31234 and 31129 are seen stabled at London Liverpool Street station awaiting their next turn of duty on 7 June 1975.

Left: 47160 with headcode 1K22 is seen at London Liverpool Street station working the 16:30 service to Yarmouth Vauxhall on 7 June 1975.

03109 shunts parcel vans at Ipswich station on 10 June 1975.

On 10 June 1975, 47150 heads a freightliner train from Felixstowe south through Ipswich station.

Right: 37247 heads a tank train (possibly the gas condensate tanks from North Walsham) south through Ipswich station to Harwich Parkeston Quay on 10 June 1975.

Below: On 14 June 1975, 47010 is seen approaching Norwich station with a passenger service from London Liverpool Street, while Eastleigh Works 6B Hastings unit 1037 waits to enter for servicing after working a railtour to Yarmouth Vauxhall.

Eastleigh Works 6B Hastings Unit 1037 heads empty stock into Norwich for servicing on 14 June 1975. The Hastings line units were built at Eastleigh Works to the Hastings line gauge, which had a restricted loading gauge due to the narrow bore tunnels on the line. They entered service in 1958, and were withdrawn when the line was electrified with single track through some of the tunnels in the late 1980s.

Class 25 25120 and Class 31 31280 are seen taking on fuel at the fuelling point at Norwich after arriving with a Saturdays-only working from Derby on 14 June 1975.

31177 departs Norwich station at 12:01 with the Saturdays-only working from Chesterfield to Yarmouth Vauxhall on 14 June 1975.

Right: 31205 is seen on 14 June 1975 on the 09:54 Yarmouth Vauxhall to London Liverpool Street service. The Class 31 would come off the train at Norwich.

Below: On 14 June 1975, Class 31s 31211/31321 arrive into Yarmouth Vauxhall station with empty coaching stock from Norwich.

03018 shunts parcels vans at Yarmouth Vauxhall station on 13 June 1975.

Left: 31101 heads a passenger train from Harwich Parkeston Quay into Ely station at 14:47, bound for Peterborough on 9 June 1975.

Below: On 13 June 1975, 31114 heads a van train north into Ely, formed of 12-ton vans.

37120 is seen at Ely station, working to King's Lynn with a service from London Liverpool Street station on 9 June 1975.

Right: 31321 departs Ely station with the 15:27 King's Lynn to London Liverpool Street service on 13 June 1975.

Below: 31113 is seen on a parcels train at Spalding with the guard checking the consist before departing west on 11 June 1975.

Chapter 4
Southern Region

A wet day at London Waterloo station on 19 July 1976 sees Southern region 4-VEP EMUs 7810 and 7821 present awaiting their next working. Ordered in 1965, 194 standard four-coach 4-VEP units were built between 1967 and 1974 at British Rail's Holgate Road Carriage Works in York and numbered 7701–7894, becoming Class 423 under the train-operating processing system (TOPS).

Hampshire diesel-electric multiple-unit (DEMU) set 1111 enters Portsmouth and Southsea station with a service to Southampton on 22 June 1976. In November 1955, the Southern region ordered 18 two-coach DEMUs, to be numbered 1101–1118. These were constructed during 1957 at Eastleigh Works, principally for Portsmouth–Southampton Central–Salisbury semi-fast services and Portsmouth–Southampton Central stopping services. In 1959, due to overcrowding, centre trailers were built for 1101–1118 and the 500hp diesel engine was removed and replaced with a 600hp diesel engine.

Class 33/1 33102 is seen at Portsmouth and Southsea low-level station on 24 June 1976 with a parcels train. The line to Bournemouth was electrified in 1967, but extending electrification to Weymouth was not considered cost effective at the time (this was eventually completed in 1988), hence a locomotive fitted with push-pull equipment was required to take unpowered trailer control (TC) trailer units from Bournemouth to Weymouth and back. In total, 19 Class 33 locomotives were fitted for push-pull working and designated Class 33/1.

4-REP EMU 3008 departs Southampton Central station for London Waterloo and is about to enter Southampton tunnel just east of the station on 22 June 1976. The 4-REP units were built at British Rail's York Carriage Works between 1966 and 1967 to a standard 1963 BR (Southern) EMU design and were formed of two driving motor second standard saloons (DMSOs) each side of a trailer brake first corridor (TBFK) and a trailer buffet (TRB). The DMSOs were new build but the TFBK was a converted loco-hauled Mk1 composite coach and the TRB from Mk1 loco-hauled restaurant/buffets and numbered 3001–3011. Another four were built in 1974 and numbered 3012–3015.

Class 423 4-VEP EMU 7701 approaches Southampton Central station with a service from London Waterloo on 22 June 1976.

Class 74 electro-diesel 74002 heads a short freight west through Southampton Central station on 24 June 1976. Ten Class 71 straight electric locomotives, built in Doncaster Works between 1958 and 1960, were deemed surplus to requirement in the South Eastern Division and were converted to Class 74s at Crewe Works. The alterations converted these locos into another electro-diesel type with 2,550hp on electric and 650hp on diesel. They were required for ocean liner traffic and worked into Southampton docks. They were introduced into traffic from late 1967 and withdrawn within ten years as they proved rather unreliable. 74002 was withdrawn following collision damage in June 1977.

47254 departs Southampton Central station with the 10:00 service to York on 24 June 1976.

4-REP EMU 3004 with 4TCs (trailer cars) 409/405 arrives into Southampton Central station from Bournemouth with a working to London Waterloo on 29 June 1976. Note the signal gantry at the west end of the station. 4TCs were converted from Mk1 coaching stock built between 1950 and 1960, conversion being done at York carriage works. 28 4TCs numbered 401–428 were built along with four 4TC push-pull buffet cars numbered 429–434 and four 3TCs numbered 301–304.

Western Class 52 D1022 named *Western Sentinel* heads a rake of empty 16-ton stone wagons north through Salisbury station bound for Westbury and Merehead quarry on 22 June 1976. In total, 74 Westerns with hydraulic transmission were built between 1961 and 1964, 35 at Swindon works and 39 at Crewe works. D1022 was constructed at Swindon works and completed in July 1963, withdrawn in January 1977 and scrapped at Swindon works in December 1978.

Left: 08387 shunts a single 16-ton wagon through Salisbury station and into the yards at the north end of the station on 22 June 1976.

Below: 33033 heads the 14:36 Salisbury to London Waterloo train out of Salisbury station, having arrived at 14:21 from Exeter St David's on 22 June 1976. In total, 98 Class 33s were built at BRCW Smethwick between 1960 and 1962 to an enlarged version of the existing Class 26 design. D6586–D6597 were built with a narrower body to meet the Hastings line gauge, becoming Class 33/2s under TOPS.

Above: 33112 heads a short freight from the north through Salisbury station on 22 June 1976.

Right: 33021 heads a ballast train east out of Salisbury station as Hampshire 3H DEMU 1101 waits to depart with the 15:45 service to Portsmouth Harbour on 22 June 1976.

Fareham station features in this photo taken on 23 June 1976, with former Hastings 2H DEMU 1121 waiting to depart with a working to Eastleigh via Botley. A second batch of 2H units were built as two-car units in 1958 at Eastleigh works and remained as two-car sets until 1979.

Above: A general view of the yard and station at Eastleigh, with former Hastings 2H DEMU 1121 at the station after arrival from Fareham via Botley on 23 June 1976.

Left: 09025 in faded BR green livery is seen shunting the yard at Eastleigh on 23 June 1976. Stabled by the station are 73126, 33009 and 73101. In total, 43 Class 73/1s were built by English Electric at the Vulcan Foundry, Newton-le-Willows, Lancashire, classified as JBs between 1965 and 1967. Several of these locomotives are still at work today, owned by GB Railfreight.

33118 heads a short intermodal bound for Southampton west through Eastleigh station on 23 June 1976.

Above: Class 423 4-VEP EMU 7705 is seen at Eastleigh station with a train for London Waterloo on 23 June 1976.

Right: 74001 heads an eastbound parcels train formed of a mixture of BR ex-Southern Region designs at Eastleigh station on 23 June 1976.

Class 73 73113 and Class 33 33109 head an MGR coal train loaded with imported coal probably from Southampton Eastern Docks or Northam, through Eastleigh station to Didcot Power Station on 23 June 1976.

07012 shunts a parcels van at Bournemouth station on 24 June 1976. The Class 07 are 0-6-0 diesel-electric shunters built by Ruston & Hornsby of Lincoln in 1962, for the Southern Region of British Rail. In total, 14 were built, primarily for use in Southampton Docks and latterly Eastleigh Works, all being withdrawn by 1977. Seven are preserved including, 07012 in BR green livery at Barrow Hill.

33107 is seen coupled to 4TCs 405/414 at Weymouth station with the 14:38 to London Waterloo on 24 June 1976. The Class 33 will propel the 4TCs as far as Bournemouth, where it will come off, after which a 4-REP EMU will couple to the 4TCs to work the train to London Waterloo.

33105 is seen stabled in front of empty Mk1 stock at Weymouth station on 24 June 1976.

On 24 June 1976, 47131 is seen stabled on a set of Mk1 stock at Weymouth station with its return working on a summer-only service.

33116 heads the Channel Islands boat train from London Waterloo down through the streets of Weymouth to Weymouth Quay station on 24 June 1976. This was the last remaining street tramway on BR, with a 4mph restriction; a shunter walked in front to stop traffic. A locomotive working on the tramway had to carry a warning bell and a flashing light. Just recently, after several years out of use, the tracks of the street tramway were removed.

Above: 73005 speeds a parcels train nonstop through Havant station towards London on 25 June 1976. Six Class 73/0s were built at Eastleigh Works and introduced into traffic in 1962, classified as JAs; they provided 1,600hp on electric power and 600hp on diesel power.

Left: 73111 is seen on a Brighton-bound parcels train at Worthing station on 25 June 1976.

Class 414 2-HAP EMUs 6070/6069 are seen working a coastway service at Worthing station on 25 June 1976. The 2-HAP EMUs were built between 1956 and 1963; these two units were among the third batch of units built and along with the second batch, were built to the newer standard Mk1 coach profile at BR's Eastleigh Works. All were withdrawn by 1995.

Class 486 EMU 034 is seen at Ryde Esplanade station on a working to Shanklin, Isle of Wight, on 21 June 1976. The line to Shanklin from Ryde was worked by steam locomotives until 1966, when it was closed for third-rail electrification at 630v DC, re-opening on 20 March 1967. BR Class 485 and 486 EMUs were originally built between 1923 and 1931 for the London Electric Railway as its standard tube stock. Six three-car sets purchased by BR were refurbished at Stewarts Lane depot, Battersea, during 1966 and 1967 and classified as 451s, then later as 486s, and numbered 031–036. Six four-car sets were also refurbished at Stewarts Lane depot and classified as 452s, then later as 485s and numbered 041–046. All were withdrawn in 1992.

Class 486 EMU 035 is seen leaving Sandown station for Shanklin on 21 June 1976.

Above: Class 05 0-6-0 DM shunter 05001 is seen stabled with an engineering train in the siding at Sandown on 21 June 1976. These shunters were built by Hunslet Engine Company between 1955 and 1961. D2554 transferred to the Isle of Wight in 1966 to aid with the electrification of the Shanklin line and was retained for engineering duties; it was renumbered to 05001 under TOPS. It was withdrawn in 1985 and sold to the Isle of Wight steam railway.

Left: Class 485 EMU 043, coupled to Class 486 EMU 033, is seen at Shanklin station, waiting to depart for Ryde Pier Head station, with the signal box in the background on 21 June 1976.

On 26 June 1976, 73112 heads a rake of Mk1 stock west out of London Waterloo station, with possibly a Southampton boat train working.

Chapter 5

Western Region

Western Class 52 D1012 named *Western Firebrand* is seen awaiting its departure time at London Paddington station on 5 April 1974. The last four Westerns were withdrawn in February 1977.

D1045 *Western Viscount*, with headcode 8E38, is stabled on a tank train in Acton yard on 5 April 1974.

Above: Hymek Class 35 D7028 works into Acton yard from the west with empty stone wagons on 5 April 1974. The Class 35 Hymek was a Type 3 built with hydraulic transmission and a Bristol-Siddeley/Maybach MD870 engine. In total, 101 were built by Beyer Peacock (Hymek) Ltd between 1961 and 1964. The locomotives were withdrawn between 1971 and 1975.

Left: D1067 named *Western Druid* with headcode 7V45 heads a freight, possibly from Temple Mill yard to Severn Tunnel Junction, west through Ealing Broadway station on 5 April 1974. Note the London Underground trains.

Class 47 1927, in original BR two-tone green livery with headcode 4V33, heads a freight train west through Ealing Broadway station on 5 April 1974.

Pressed Steel Class 121 single-car DMU W55021 and trailer car W56286 are seen departing Ealing Broadway station on a Greenford branch working on 5 April 1974. These units were introduced into service in 1960. The Class 121 single-car units lasted into privatisation of the railways with Silverlink; the last two units were taken out of service in 2017 with Chiltern Railways.

Right: 37185 heads a ballast train of dogfish wagons east through Reading station towards London on 19 April 1975.

Below: 31257 on steam-heated Mk1 stock is seen at Reading station working the 1A48 16:15 Worcester Shrub Hill to London Paddington service on 19 April 1975.

D1046 named *Western Marquis* is seen at Reading station, working the 1B19 17:30 London Paddington to Penzance service on 19 April 1975.

25260 is seen heading a long rake of 12-ton vans north, approaching Oxford station on 6 June 1978.

31217 heads empty steel wagons north, approaching Cheltenham Spa station with the twin tracks of the closed Honeybourne line still visible in the right of the photo on 6 June 1978. The line from Honeybourne to Cheltenham via Toddington (Great Western Railways Cheltenham to Stratford-upon-Avon to Birmingham line) was run down over the years and finally closed in 1976 after a derailment damaged a section of track. The Gloucestershire and Warwickshire Railway now operates part of the line from Cheltenham Racecourse to Broadway.

45136, with headcode 8M65, heads a coal train north through Cheltenham Spa station on 3 October 1974.

Right: On 2 October 1974, 47239, with headcode 6M32, heads northbound china clay hoods to Stoke through Cheltenham Spa station.

Below: 37274 is seen on a westbound parcels train at Swindon station on 5 June 1978. The Class 37 had earlier picked up more parcels vans brought in by 37251.

A misformed Great Western Railway (GWR) High Speed Train (HST) set with Power Car 43019 leading (Eastern Region Power Car 43063 of set 254004 on rear) heads west through Bath to Bristol Temple Meads on 9 June 1978. On 4 October 1976, a partial HST service was introduced on the Western Region between London Paddington and the South Wales Main Line. By May 1977, the full complement of 27 sets (253001–027) was operating the lines to South Wales and Bristol.

Class 37s 37192/247 head a loaded stone train from the Mendip quarries into the yard at Bristol Parkway on 5 June 1978. After leaving the loaded wagons in the yard, both Class 37s ran light to Bristol (Bath Road) depot. Bristol Parkway station opened in 1972 as a park-and-ride station.

On 5 June 1978, 50009 named *Conqueror* shunts a parcels van at Bristol Temple Meads station. 50009 was named *Conqueror* at Laira depot on 8 May 1978.

Above: 47077 named *North Star* is seen with a long rake of Mk1 stock, departing Weston-super-Mare station with the 14:02 1C58 Paignton to Swansea service on 3 June 1978. This Class 47 is still active today, and is currently at the North Yorkshire Moors Railway, on hire from the Diesel & Electric Preservation Group.

Right: 45002 is seen approaching Weston-super-Mare station with the late running 10:40 1V85 Manchester Piccadilly to Paignton service on 3 June 1978.

A GWR HST set, misformed with power car 43029 of set 253014 leading and Eastern Region power car 43062 of set 254004 on the rear, is seen on single line south of Weston-super-Mare station on empty stock working on 3 June 1978. The train is about to head back into the station to work the 16:45 service to London Paddington.

25224 is seen with Mk1 stock at Newport station with a service for Cardiff from Crewe on 8 June 1978. Newport station has considerably changed since this photo was taken, with an additional platform now constructed, electrification throughout and the station itself has had a rebuild.

Left: Class 37 37210, with headcode 8Z19, and Class 47 47449 double-head a loaded MGR coal train east through Newport station, possibly bound for Llanwern steelworks, and are seen exiting Hillfield railway tunnels on 2 October 1974.

Below: 47506, with a headcode of 6Z64, leads covered steel wagons west through Newport station on 2 October 1974.

Brush Class 53 1200, named *Falcon,* heads a freight west through Newport station on 2 October 1974. This locomotive was built in 1961 by Brush Traction as a single prototype diesel-electric design of Co-Co arrangement, which would be lighter than earlier Co-Co arrangements such as the Peak classes (Class 44/45/46) and was fitted with two Maybach MD655 engines and numbered D0280. It operated on the Eastern Region until 1965 when it moved to the Western Region. It was renumbered by British Railways to 1200, withdrawn in October 1975 and scrapped in May 1976.

Right: On 3 October 1974, 08109 shunts one 16-ton coal wagon with a guard's van east through Newport station, passing the site of Godfrey Road stabling point, which was closed around 2006 and is now occupied by a new station entrance and car park, built during a rebuild of the station.

Below: 08189 shunts parcels vans at Cardiff Central station on 2 October 1974.

Above: 47530 heads empty coal wagons east approaching Cardiff Central station on 2 October 1974. Note that one of the 16-ton coal wagons appears to have a hot box or dragging brakes with smoke being emitted.

Left: GWR HST set 253017 is seen at Swansea station with a passenger service for London Paddington on 7 June 1978. Just visible is 37184 stabled on a parcels train at the station.

Below: D1072 named *Western Glory* is seen at Taunton station with 1A29, the 05:05 Penzance to London Paddington passenger service on 14 June 1974. The middle island platform was not in use at the time.

Above: 47342 is seen on the rear of milk tanks at Exeter St David's station on 17 June 1974.

Right: 50027 heads a passenger train for London Paddington at Exeter St David's station on 17 June 1974.

33020, having arrived earlier on Mk1 stock, is seen at Exeter St David's station with a passenger service from London Waterloo on 12 June 1974.

Above: 46024 heads 6B64, the Plymouth Friary to Exeter Riverside freight, into Exeter station on 12 June 1974. Note the signal gantry and water tower in the background.

Left: A view of Exeter stabling point on 12 June 1974 sees 25306, 33023 and an unidentified Class 31 present. After the last locomotive based at 83C left in 1963, the shed area was kept as a fuelling and stabling point for locomotives and DMUs and was used for many years without a roof, as seen in this photograph. In 1980, a new covered maintenance area was built, further new facilities were added in 2011 and a new train maintenance depot was completed in 2021.

08394 brings cement tanks off the incline from Exeter Central station heading to the yard beyond Exeter St David's station on 12 June 1974.

Above: D1052 *Western Viceroy* heads a southbound passenger train past the signal box out of Exeter St David's station on 17 June 1974.

Right: 25326 heads china clay hood wagons into Barnstaple station, possibly from Torrington on 13 June 1974. The Torrington branch closed to passenger trains in 1965 and to freight in 1982.

47231 heads 1E37, the return of the 'Devonian', from Paignton to Leeds with Mk1 stock at Dawlish on 17 June 1974.

Above: On 17 June 1974, D1031 named *Western Rifleman,* with a very smoky exhaust, heads 1A69, the 08:35 Penzance to London Paddington, past the holidaymakers at Dawlish seafront.

Left: 47464 is seen heading a freight east along the seafront wall at Teignmouth on 11 June 1974.

With a parcels van on the rear, 50009 heads 1A59, the 09:50 Plymouth to London Paddington service, along the seafront wall and cliffs at Teignmouth on 15 June 1974.

Above: D1059 named *Western Empire* heads 1V34, the 07:50 Kensington Olympia to St Austell Motorail train, approaching Teignmouth station on 15 June 1974.

Right: On 11 June 1974, D1009 named *Western Invader* heads 1A05, the 11:55 Paignton to London Paddington service, along the seafront at Teignmouth.

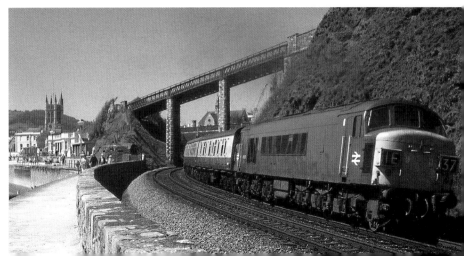

45115 heads train 1E37, the return of the 'Devonian', from Paignton to Leeds at Teignmouth on 11 June 1974.

Above: D1048 named *Western Lady* leads 7V53, the Stoke to St Blazey china clay empties, through Newton Abbot station on 10 June 1974.

Left: 45015 with headcode 4M07 heads a passenger train, probably bound for Manchester Piccadilly, at Newton Abbot station on 10 June 1974.

A Gloucester Railway Carriage & Wagon Company Class 119 DMU P588 set formed of 51079/59437/51107 departs Newton Abbot station under the GWR signal gantry for Paignton on 10 June 1974. The Class 119s were based on the Swindon Class 120s but with a Derby-designed cab. The units were introduced into service in 1958 and the last vehicles were withdrawn in 1995.

D1029 named *Western Legionnaire* heads 1B29, the 12:30 London Paddington to Paignton service, at Torquay station on 15 June 1974.

D1055 named *Western Advocate*, D1069 named *Western Vanguard* and D1037 named *Western Empress*, all with their engines running, shunt a parcels van at Laira depot in Plymouth on 18 June 1974.

Other books you might like:

Britain's Railways Series,
Vol. 52

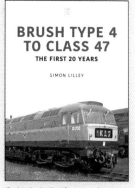

Britain's Railways Series,
Vol. 44

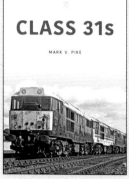

Britain's Railways Series,
Vol. 50

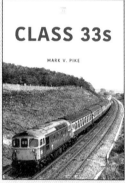

Britain's Railways Series,
Vol. 40

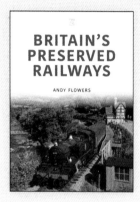

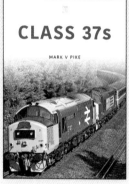

Britain's Railways Series,
Vol. 23

For our full range of titles please visit:
shop.keypublishing.com/books